Model Boat Building

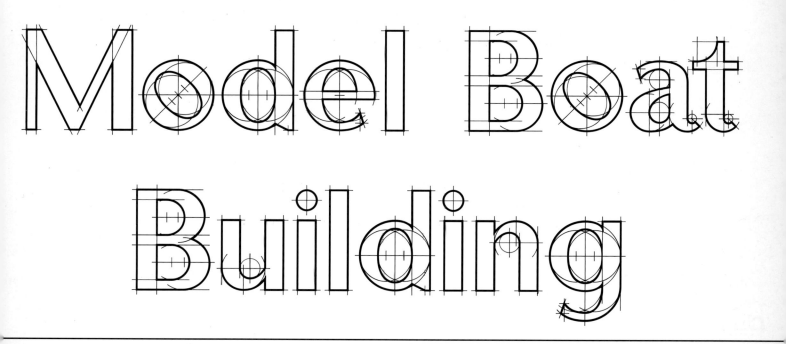

The Menhaden Steamer

Steve Rogers & Patricia Staby Rogers

Model Boat Building

The Menhaden Steamer

Steve Rogers & Patricia Staby Rogers

Schiffer Publishing Ltd

4880 Lower Valley Road, Atglen, PA 19310 USA

Published by Schiffer Publishing Ltd.
4880 Lower Valley Road
Atglen, PA 19310
Phone: (610) 593-1777; Fax: (610) 593-2002
E-mail: Schifferbk@aol.com
Please visit our web site catalog at
www.schifferbooks.com
This book may be purchased from the publisher.
Include $3.95 for shipping.
Please try your bookstore first.
We are interested in hearing from authors
with book ideas on related subjects.
You may write for a free catalog.

In Europe, Schiffer books are distributed by
Bushwood Books
6 Marksbury Ave.
Kew Gardens
Surrey TW9 4JF England
Phone: 44 (0) 208 392-8585; Fax: 44 (0) 208 392-9876
E-mail: Bushwd@aol.com
Free postage in the U.K., Europe; air mail at cost.
Try your bookstore first

Book Design by Anne Davidsen
Type set in Rubino / Lithograph / Duth 801

ISBN: 0-7643-1070-4
Printed in China

INTRODUCTION

Over and over again I was asked if I built a model of a "fish boat," which is the vernacular for a menhaden boat. I hadn't. I didn't know much about them, since I concentrate on smaller working boats which are less complicated. My major concern was the lack of good information. I knew I would need hull lines, construction details, and drawings and photos of the equipment. There are a lot of boats whose construction follows a formula or has certain dimensional ratios, but the menhaden steamers are not among them. They are double framed, heavily built offshore boats. Their builders probably worked from half hulls. There may be blueprints around, but, to date, none have surfaced from the shipyards that built these boats. The general arrangement, however, is almost unchanged since 1880.

After about the fourth inquiry and the realization that Lewes, Delaware, was the home port for a major fleet of the menhaden steamers, I could avoid it no longer. I started gathering information, including some from a group of locals attending a wildlife show in Whitestone, Virginia. They had either been in the menhaden business themselves or their families had. The conversation I had with them was enlightening about how the ships were used in purse seining for menhaden, but less informative about the kind of details I would need to build a model boat.

Well, about a year later an envelope arrived from Louisiana. Inside was a thirty year old plan of a "fishboat." The plan was designed to produce a radio controlled balsa wood model of a menhaden steamer. The model was described as a "typical fishboat," but in fact was based on an actual boat called the "Helen Euphane." The hull lines and general arrangement were taken while the boat was located in Port Monmouth, New Jersey. The "Helen Euphane" was then owned by the J. Howard Smith Company of Lewes, and Port Monmouth was one of their plants. Although the plan was brief in terms of detail, what I needed to know was there, and a nice model could be built.

I built my first model using the plan scale of 5/16"=1'0", resulting in a large, impressive model. The details you didn't see on the plan emerged on the model and made it very attractive. I was so pleased with the result that I couldn't resist showing it to my neighbor. He actually worked as an engineer on the menhaden fleet and, to my surprise, remembered the "Helen Euphane." Although Ranny had been assigned to a larger steel boat called "Green Lane," the "Helen Euphane" and its crew docked at the same pier and he knew the boat well.

In one sense he loved the model. Someone had finally built a model of his beloved fishboats. He told me it was "a fine model, Steve, but...[big but]...I don't remember it that way." Next he proceeded to point out all the ways in which the model deviated from his memory of the "Helen

Euphane." I had to suppress my upwelling resentment and realize that I was being given a golden opportunity that few model builders experience - the chance to examine a model with someone who didn't just know the boat, but loves it as well and provides the important details and insights about it.

As it turns out, the "Helen Euphane" deserves this level of effort because it was a very old boat and served a long and useful life. At the time it sank and was broken up, it was over ninety years old. It was built in 1902 by the Tull Shipyard on the banks of the Pocomoke River in Pocomoke City, Maryland. During both World Wars it was taken over by the Navy and patrolled for submarines. Most of the remainder of its life it purse seined for menhaden. The "Helen Euphane" spent its last years as a house boat in West Ocean City, Maryland.

My neighbor Ranny Hudson's comments motivated me to do some more research. Angus Murdock at the Reedville Fisherman's Museum was kind enough to send me copies of photos and a painting - all of the "Helen Euphane." Other friends sent me a list of all the boats owned by the Smith family and the disposition of each after the company sold out in the 1960s. Don George of Dahlgren, Virginia, who keeps pictures, technical data, and histories of over 500 original menhaden boats sent me information on several other Smith boats that showed up in photos of the plant.

One of the photos shows the "Helen Euphane" just after its launching in 1902. Although the photo is grainy and inadequate for fine detail, it shows the important superstructure and engine stack dimensions and placement. Another picture clearly shows the round stern and railing. A copy of the painting clearly shows the fine details only hinted at in the photographs. Ranny was right.

When it sank in 1994, the "Helen Euphane" was the last of hundreds of steam and diesel-powered fishboats that worked the east coast from Maine to the Gulf of Mexico. It was a huge industry with thousands of people working in it. In 1953 the port of Lewes landed the most tonnage of fish anywhere in the country. Today the boats are gone, the plants mostly closed or torn down, and the men retired. The industry survives today in Reedville, Virginia, Beaufort, North Carolina, and the Gulf of Mexico, but they use converted Navy minesweepers instead of boats designed for menhaden fishing. (One of several exceptions is the "Green Lane" which was a fairly modern boat in the 1960s and probably is still working.) Several steel boats built in the fifties have been converted to clamming and may still be working.

SOME NOTES ON TERMINOLOGY

I find myself having the very bad habit of creating "pet names" for items that, after enough usage, I begin to believe are correct. Some of the problem stems from the construction method we are using for this model. Most boats have a heavy longitudinal structure inside the hull called the **keelson.** Attached to keelson forward is the **stem**. Aft is the **sternpost.** The bottom of the hull that streamlines the hull to the sternpost and the keel is called the **deadwood.** In some ships the actual deadwood is planked over and hidden within the hull. In our boat the deadwood is external and fills the triangular space between the keel and the hull. The **false keel** is a space holder, for our purposes, and gives the illusion of a **rabbet**, which is a shallow groove the length of the keel, deadwood, and stem into which the **garboard** (first) plank and on the stem, the hood ends (the trimmed and fitted ends) on the planking lay. In our model there is no keelson and no rabbet, only the appearance of one. Instead of a rabbetted stem we use a linered stemed which has two components, one inside and the other outside. This approach greatly simplifies the planking process.

You may already be familiar with most of the terms being used here, but here is an explanation for several of them.

forward:	the front end of the boat
aft:	the stern end
port:	the left side (looking forward)
starboard:	the right side (looking forward)
ribs:	structural support for the planking-like frames
rim log:	a structural component that supports the stern to which the bottom planks and stern planks are attached. Used on elliptical or round sterns
packing:	semi-structural pieces that "pack out" and provide support for fastening of planks
hanging ribs:	ribs that receive planks but are not attached to the stem or the keel
cheek pieces:	actually a hanging rib, only wider. Planks attach to it and the stem liner. It adds strength to the bow
sheer:	the highest point of the hull
deck line:	on the inside of the hull this is the top of the deck surface
stanchion:	a support for a rail. It can be metal, for metal railing, or wood.

davit:	a sort of crane that allows you to lift or launch boats over the side of the hull and carries them while underway
side lights:	the red and green lights on the sides of the ship
ventilators:	bell shaped metal hoods that direct airflow below decks or into a system
hawse lips:	a protective flange around a hole in the hull through which anchor line and chain will pass into its locker
fairlead:	a groove, guide, or fitting through which a rope passes
scupper:	openings in the bulwarks (hull above the deck) that allow water to drain quickly

MATERIALS FOR YOUR MODEL

Most of this boat was built with a 1" x 10" x 10' piece of very good white pine. If I had not found this particular piece of board, I would have used some of my sugar pine. I usually cut the board into "stock" ahead of time, storing it in a "rack" according to size. For this boat I cut a sufficient amount of my usual sizes, except for the planks, which I cut 60" long x 3/8" wide x 3/32" thick. This is simply for convenience since we know there weren't any 100' long plank used on these boats. Any other visible component was cut to scale dimensions (1/4" x 1/4" = 6" x 6") and to length when called for on the plan. Joints are usually scarphed to minimize their appearance.

The ribs and other bent shapes, such as fenders and cabin front framing, were made from poplar and soaked in ammonia. I purchased a piece of poplar, 1" x 3" x 36" and sawed it into the various sizes. My ammonia reservoir only holds 24" long pieces so that's the longest length. Stock for the ribes was cut 1/4" x 1/8" x 24". Stock for the stem liner and cheek pieces were 1/2" x 1/8" x 24" and stock for the forward curved sections of the cabin and pilot house were cut 1/8" x 1/16" x 24".

The remainder of assorted trim pieces, stops, supports, and more I got from my little "lumber rack," but the requirements can be determined from the plan.

ADDITIONAL READING

I have written four previous books that you may wish to refer to as you build the menhaden steamer. They will provide a good introduction to model boat building. All are available from bookstores or by contacting Schiffer Publishing at 4880 Lower Valley Road, Atglen, PA 19382. Their phone is 610-593-1777 or they are on the internet at www.schifferbooks.com.

For additional reading about the menhaden industry I suggest *The Men All Singing* by John Frye and published by the Donning Co.

For anyone who would like a little more information about the construction of wooden ships from this time period, I strongly recommend *Wooden Ship Building* by Charles Desmond, published by the Vestal Press. The book, originally published in 1919, thoroughly discusses shipbuilding as practiced early in this century. Particularly useful are several Lloyd's of London minimum specification for scantlings (frames, beams, posts, keels, keelsons, etc.) for each tonnage range.

SHIPS FITTINGS

I buy whatever I can. Availability is a problem everywhere. For this model I purchased the portholes, hawse lips and stanchions (both metal and wood). I made my propeller but bought the anchor, searchlight, and turnbuckles. I used nylon kite line for some of the rigging but purchased various line and chain for the rest. I looked for davits in 1/2" scale, but couldn't find any, so I was forced to solder up my own from soft copper tubing.

Here is a list of some of my sources:

The Dromedary Ship Modelers Center
6324 Belton Drive
El Paso, TX 79912

Bluejacket Ship Crafters
Dept 483, Box 425
Stockton Springs, ME 04981

Micro Mark
340 Snyder Ave.
Berkeley Heights, NJ 07922

A.J. Fisher Inc.
1002 Etowah Ave.
Royal Oak, MI 48067

The Hobby Shop
Rt. 13
Seaford, DE 19973

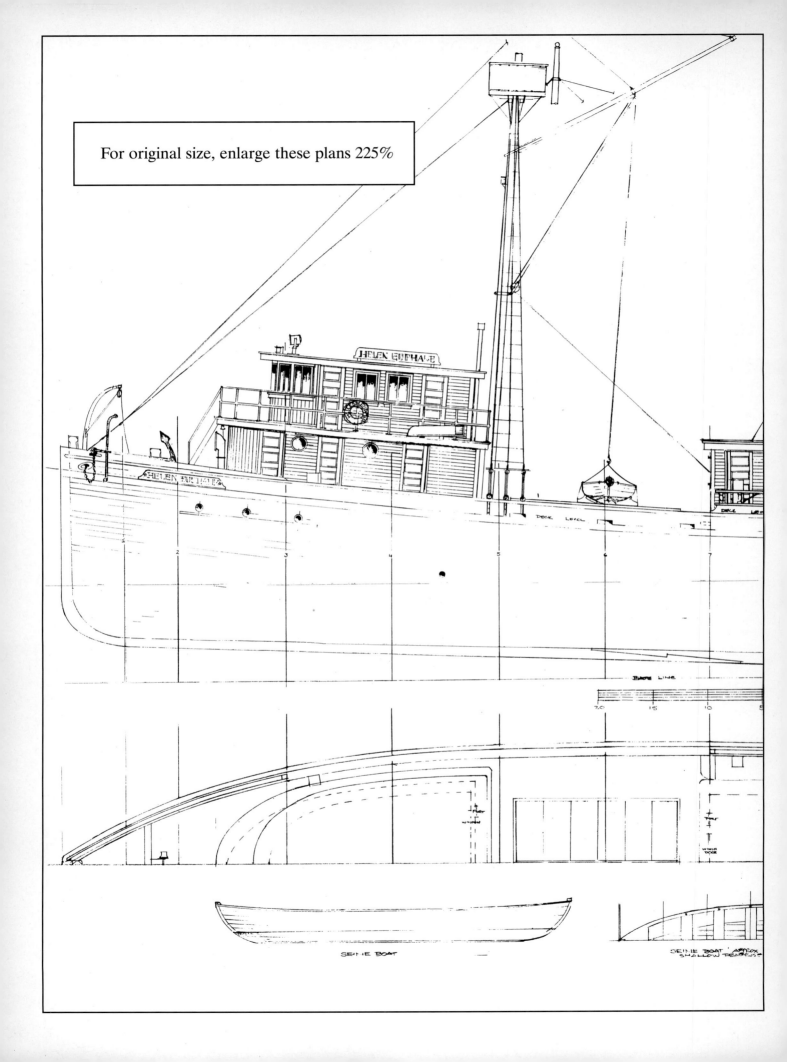

For original size, enlarge these plans 225%

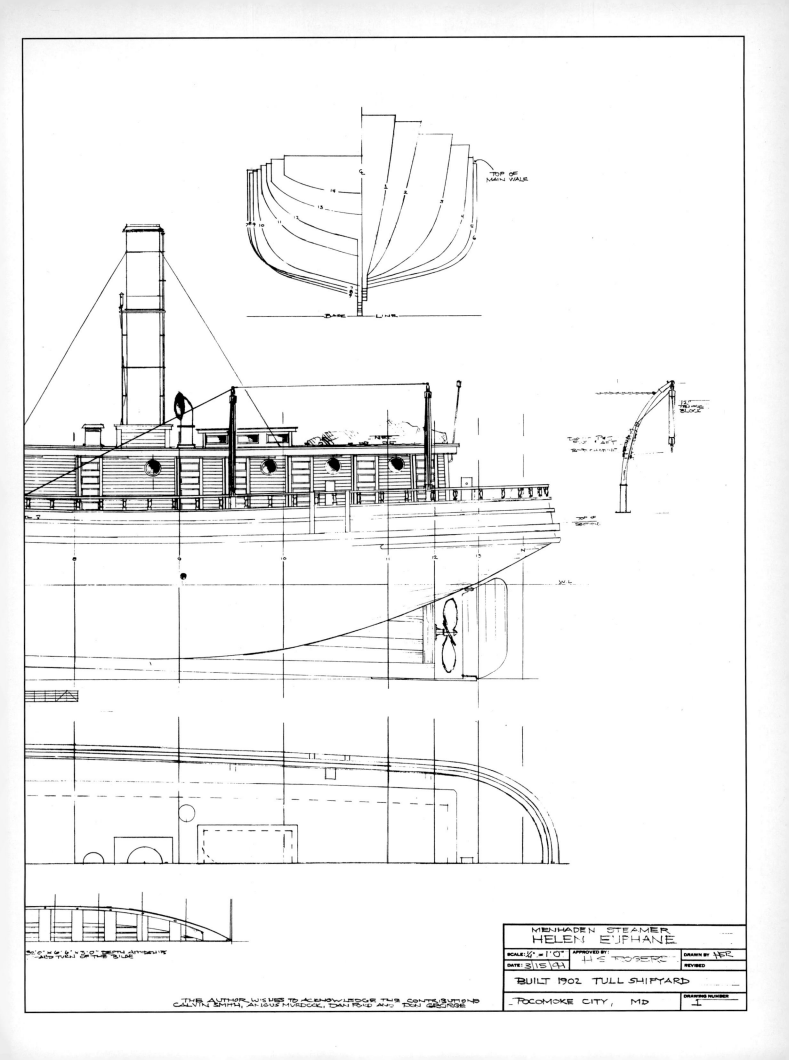

TOP OF
MAIN WALE

14
13
12
7 8 9 10 11
6
1 2 3 4 5 6

BASE LINE

TOP OF SECTION

W.L.

12" TRIPLE
BLOCK

DEPTH AFT
RABBIT LINE?

8 9 10 11 12 13 14

30'0" × 6'6" × 3'0" DEPTH AMIDSHIPS
AND TURN OF THE BILGE

THE AUTHOR WISHES TO ACKNOWLEDGE THE CONTRIBUTIONS
CALVIN SMITH, ANGUS MURDOCK, DAN FORD AND DON GEORGE

MENHADEN STEAMER		
HELEN E. PHANE		
SCALE: ¼" = 1'0"	APPROVED BY: H S ROGERS	DRAWN BY HER
DATE: 3/15/91		REVISED
BUILT 1902 TULL SHIPYARD		
POCOMOKE CITY, MD		DRAWING NUMBER 1

BUILDING THE BOAT

I went further into the history than I meant to, so let's move on and build the model. The process is basically simple. Using the lines provided in the plan, you will build a solid wood master of the hull. The only difference is that this master will be 1/4" smaller all around. The lines are drawn to the outside of the hull but the master has to allow for the thickness of the ribs and planks. The model I am building is in 1/2" scale so it will be large. You can choose another scale if you wish. You can do this easily by using the method illustrated here.

A bandsaw is used to saw away excess stock from a built-up sugar pine blank. Layout the lines and stations everywhere you can, and when a sawing operation removes a reference point, redraw it on the new surface. The goal is to maintain a precise relationship between the stations on the plan, the stations on your master, and the hull cross sections.

The bandsawing operation is strictly to remove excess stock, so you can get to the precise shaping of each section more quickly. One thing I do is to make a cut that removes the "minimum dead rise amidships." After the cut is made, I reattach the piece using brads or double-faced tape. When you are ready to start shaping amidships (which is where you start), it will give you a good head start.

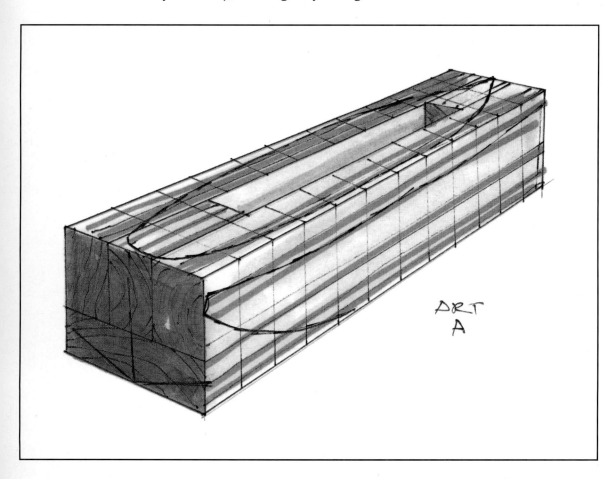

ART
A

The blank is made up of several pieces of sugar pine, glued together. The reference lines of the plan and the basic shape of the hull is drawn. When these are removed by sawing, redraw them.

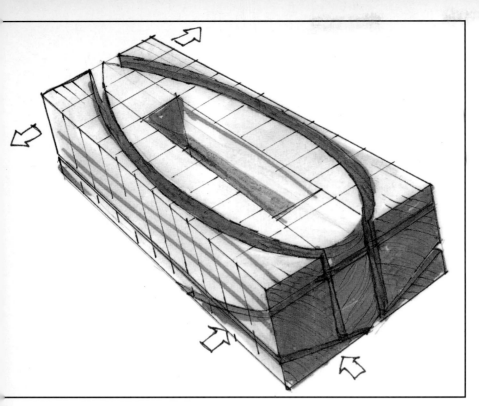

The 5 basic bandsaw cuts.

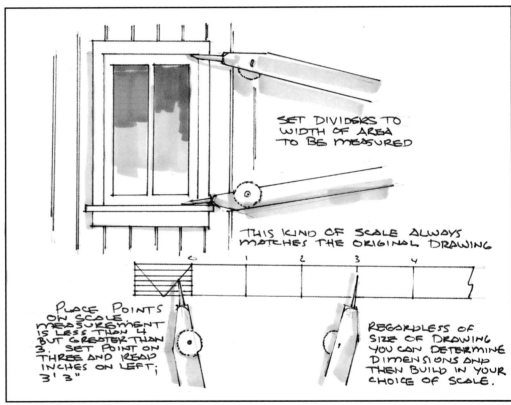

SET DIVIDERS TO WIDTH OF AREA TO BE MEASURED

THIS KIND OF SCALE ALWAYS MATCHES THE ORIGINAL DRAWING

PLACE POINTS ON SCALE. MEASUREMENT IS LESS THAN 4 BUT GREATER THAN 3. SET POINT ON THREE AND READ INCHES ON LEFT; 3' 3"

REGARDLESS OF SIZE OF DRAWING YOU CAN DETERMINE DIMENSIONS AND THEN BUILD IN YOUR CHOICE OF SCALE.

From this point on patience is necessary. Trace the cross sections onto thin plywood and check the template at each station in the plan. The goal is to create a smooth shape to the hull master that agrees with the template at each station. I use a drawknife, a small block plane, and a Sur-form tool for shaping the master to match the template. This process just takes time, so don't rush it. After you think you are done, walk away from it and come back the next day. Look for any obvious inconstancy, then sand it again and you are ready to proceed to the next step.

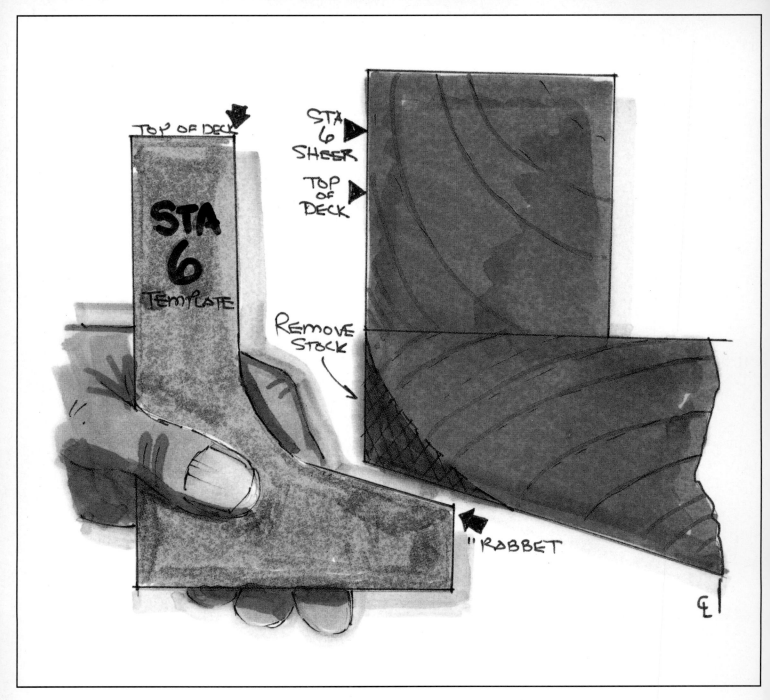

Plywood templates are used at each station to guide the shaping process.

The "ribs" that lay on the master, over which you will plank, are poplar. Cut strips 1/8" x 1/4" x 24" long. Cut some additional pieces 1/8" x 1/2" x 24" long form the stem liner.

The model I am building is in 1/2" scale and is 56" long. Since the spacing of the ribs is 1-1/2" on center, I need 40 pieces just for the ribs. Allow another twenty or so for framing around the stern and for the stern fender, and cut some finer pieces, 1/8" x 1/16" for window and deck house trim. Size will depend on your scale.

The entire assortment of ribs and miscellaneous framing is soaked in household ammonia (I use a length of sealed PVC pipe). A day is normally enough time to make it pliable. Test your pieces by bending them slowly over the master. If they do it without breaking they are ready. Apply them to the master, securing the ends with a small nail. Using a divider, scribe the location of the next rib from the previous one (your station lines will guide you). Work from the center aft, then forward. The stern planking is done with vertical staves, so the framing underneath runs horizontally. Add extra stock where the bottom meets the stern.

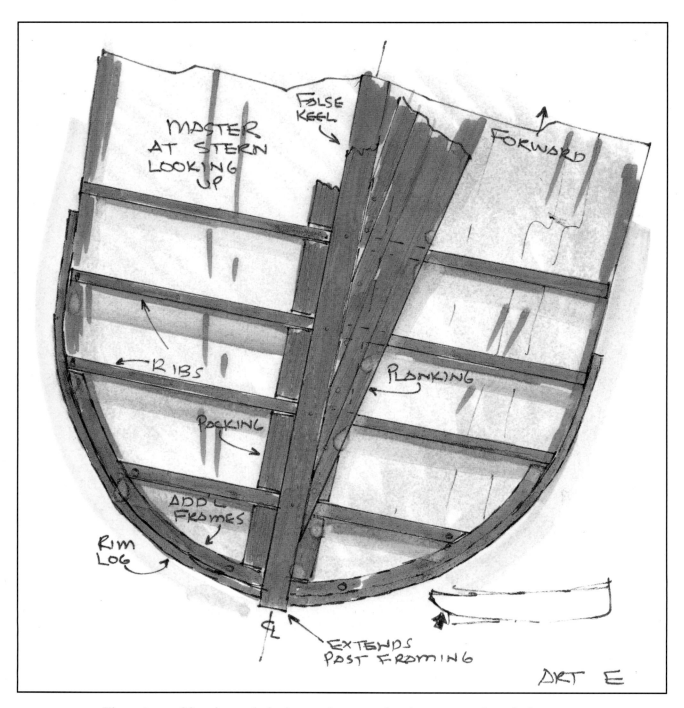

The pattern of framing and planing on the stern, showing extra stock at the bottom.

At the stem fasten multiple thicknesses to build up to a stem liner. Take the first piece down and under at least a few inches along the keel. Start the second piece about an inch closer to forward. Pin the third piece on the front face of the stem and add the cheek pieces.

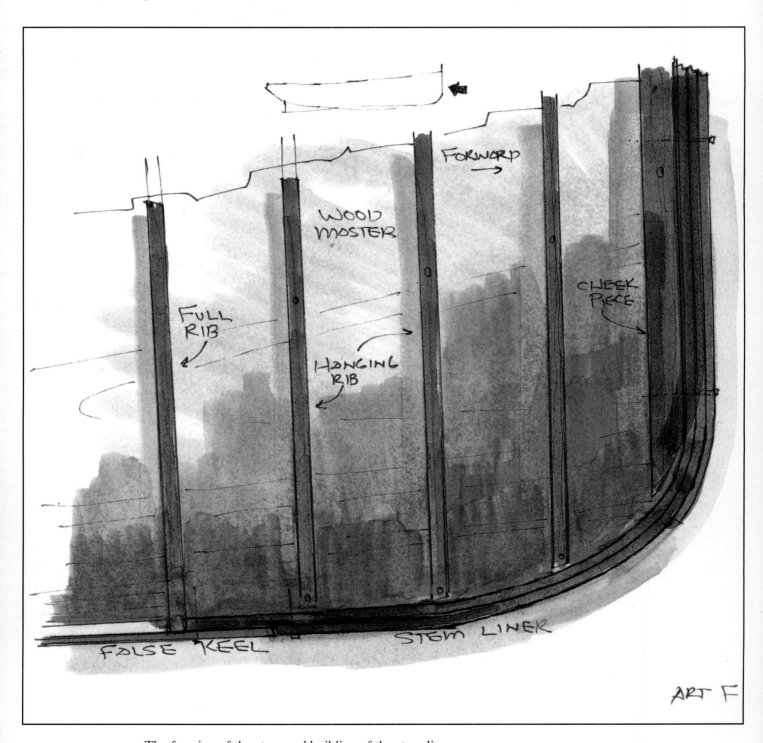

The framing of the stem and building of the stem liner.

Allow the ribs and framing to dry overnight. Carefully disassemble, then reassemble the stem assembly with glue and a few brads or pins. When this is dry, guide your knife blade along the cheek pieces to establish the correct bevel on the stem liner. Finish with a sanding block.

Using a piece of plank stock, lay in a false keel strip. It will run from the stern along the center line of the hull. Glue and fasten. When your false keel is dry, use the sanding block to fair the edges of the ribs and framing. Much sanding should not be required, but a little will help the planks lay fairer. At the stern, aft of the stern post, is an area where the planks will tail off to a point to meet the false keel. It will be necessary to pack some wide plank stock between the ribs and under the false keel to receive them. Pin, glue, and, when dry, lightly fair the packing with the sanding block. You are now ready to plank.

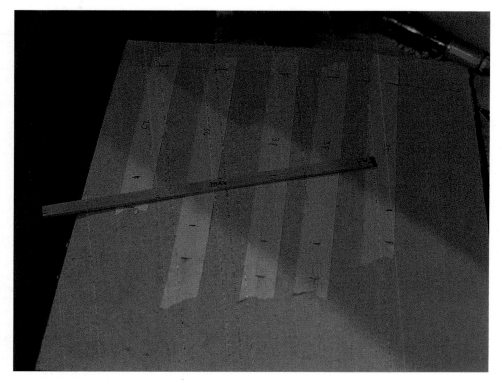

To calculate the necessary taper of the planks, measure the mold at several points using tape. The widest point on the mold represents 100% of the width of your plank (in this case 3/8"). All other measurements are then percentages. When these percentages and points are transferred to a full-length master plank, the necessary shape becomes apparent. Plane 4 to 6 planks each time and hang half on each side. Constantly recheck your measurements and make corrections as necessary.

The hull is almost completely planked. I started with the garboard (first plank at the keel) and worked toward the sheer (top edge of the hull). Nails hold the planks in place while the glue dries.

When thoroughly dry the nails are carefully pried up with a chisel and then pulled out with pliers.

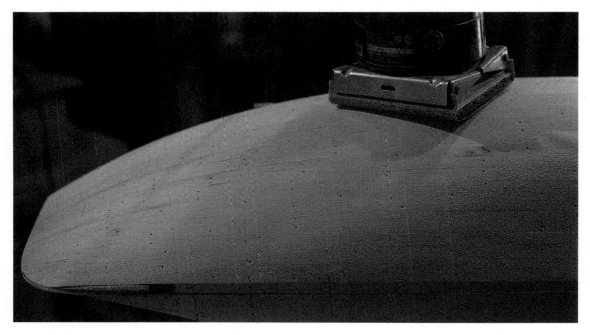

After all the nails are pulled, an orbital sander is used to rough sand the hull.
Leave it on the master for support.

Sanding and wiping briefly with clean water will remove almost all evidence
of the nails.

I never find all the nails, but I'm very careful when I glue the planks. The hull is strong enough to withstand a hidden nail or two and separates cleanly from the mold.

A slightly thinned solution of glue is mixed. It will bond the hull from the inside, finding and filling the gaps. I have placed tape over any gaps that would allow the glue to leak out.

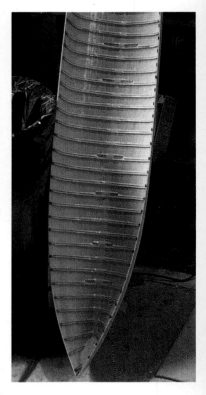

Above: Pour the mixture in and brush it thoroughly into the structure.

Right: Allow excess glue to drain into the forefoot of the hull. Once the flow stops, pour off the accumulated glue and allow the hull to dry thoroughly. I check it over as it dries to catch any glue that may ooze out of gaps or nail holes, and wipe them away from the outside of the hull. You will be astounded at the strength of the hull when it dries. Take note that there is a tendency for the hull to close inward, so check the measurement before you fit a deck beam.

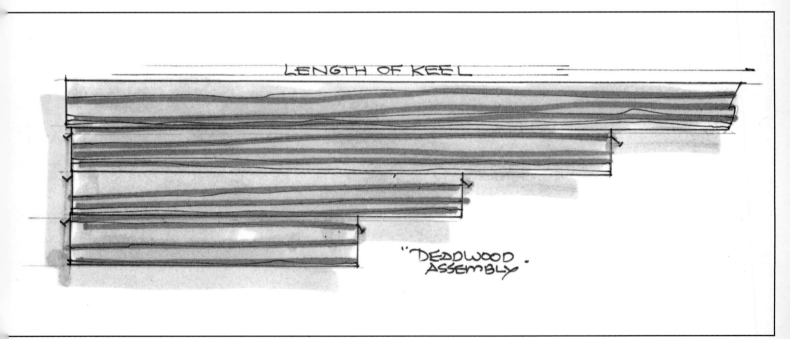

LENGTH OF KEEL

"DEADWOOD.
ASSEMBLY"

Cut stock for the sternpost and keel. Glue up the deadwood as shown and set it aside.

Fit the sternpost onto the hull.. When both the sternpost and the deadwood are dry, clamp the deadwood in place with a spring clip and scribe it to fit the hull and the sternpost.

The sternpost was left a little long to aid in the scribing process. It will be trimmed later.

Here I scribed a slightly oversized piece of white cedar to the stem. It will be rough trimmed now and finished later. Scribe pieces to fill the gap between the stem and the keel.

Refer to the plan. Add three fourths of the thickness of the deck beams to the depth of the deck below the sheer. Scribe this line across the ribs and glue a clamp in place to support the deck beams. Note: The top edge of the hull has been trimmed to the sheer line less the thickness of the cap rail.

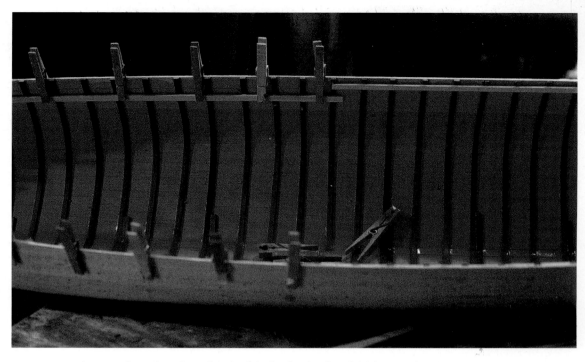

As noted on the plan, the deck is flush aft of amidships. Make the same calculations, scribe, and glue another clamp.

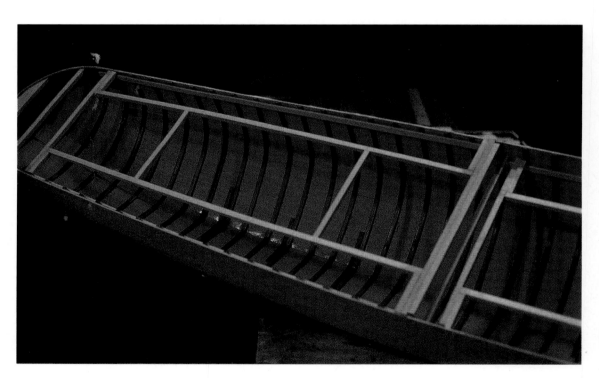

Beams and carlins for the major structures on the deck are next. The openings for the pilot and engine houses are smaller than the structure and will have a rail fastened at deck level to which the houses will be fastened.

The hold beams and carlins are larger than the opening because of the trim around the opening. The hold is an opening through the deck and the covers can be removable if you wish.

Don't forget the little foredeck. I actually got fancier than necessary under the forward cabin.

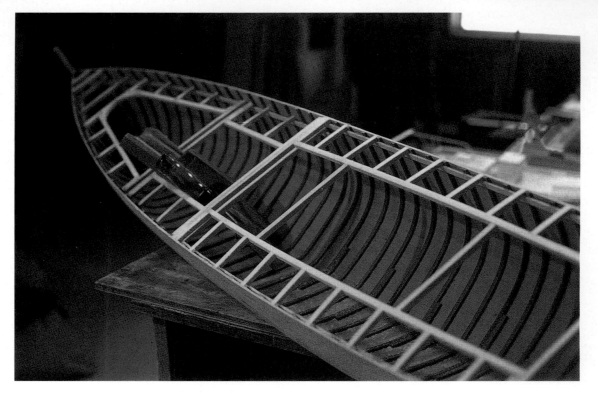

I put spreaders into the engine house opening so they would parallel the hull sides. Then I added the half beams.

Don't skimp on support that nobody sees. It makes fastening and gluing the deck faster and easier. I scribed this piece to the curve of the stern for strength and ease of gluing.

A deck crown is imparted to the beams and is about the depth of the planks. The middle third of the beams is left flat and then sanded in a smooth transition to the beam ends. The truth is that I always do this before installation, but all of a sudden I realized these things were glued in and I had forgotten. Thank God for a sharp chisel.

Scribe mid points on the major beams, the stem, and the stern.

Glue the "king plank" in place. It is usually twice to triple the normal plank width. Just make sure it is dead center and runs the length of the hull. It is your starting point for planking.

Begin planking around the hatch opening. These planks are 1/4" wide, since this is a large model. The trim piece at the forward end of the aft deck is just pinned in place for position.

Stern planking in place.

Foredeck and forward of the pilot house.

The remaining deck is fitted as closely as possible to the hull and sanded smooth.

The short pieces that are used to fill the bulkhead between the hold and the engine compartment are measured using a divider.

Ceiling planks are clamped and glued in place. Fillers were fitted between the ribs at the location of the scuppers.

Hatch framing is fitted and an inner frame is installed to hold the covers. I allowed about a 3/16" drop in this case so that the covers will be flush with the top of the hatch.

Top and bottom trim is glued and clamped in place. The remaining trim will be added in the next step. You may notice that I put in the step to the aft deck.

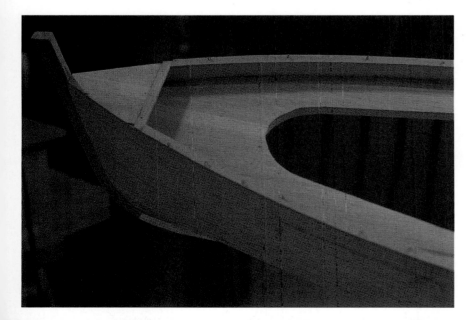

Here is where I started applying the cap rail. Next, fill the space under the foredeck. I added a stop on the deck under the beam and installed planking to seal the opening.

I usually add trim inside and out of the cap rail forward. It makes it easier to match it up with the trim on other parts of the hull. The heavy fender located at deck level has also been applied.

The fender and trim sections around the stern are comprised of poplar, soaked in ammonia, and bent to shape. Several thicknesses have been added and pinned together to dry prior to gluing.

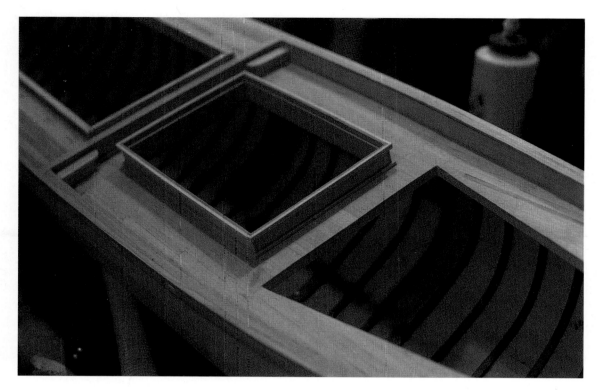

The hatch completed. Scuppers on one side opened up.

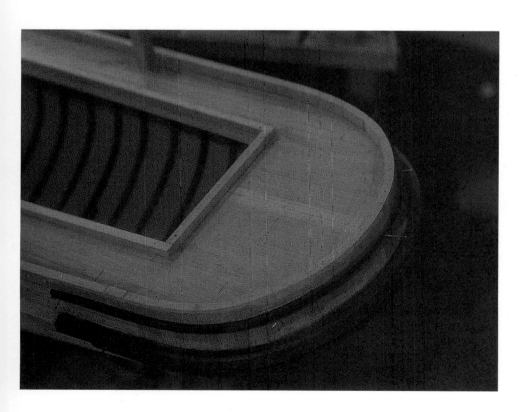

The log rail and the curved pieces that comprise the stern portion have dried and are ready to be faired

Remove the trim in order to get clear access to the outside face of the stern log rail.

Finish the inside trim forward.

This is a little jig I made to drill a hole in the stanchions for a pin. The stanchion goes head first into the jig and the drill with a very small bit creates the hole. By the way, I bought these stanchions as well as metal stanchions used around the pilot house.

A cap rail has been applied over the log rail. Pins were inserted and glued, and the stanchions were glued over the pins.

The top rail forward is a straight piece, glued and pinned to the stanchions.

The stern top rail is poplar bent around the hull master and allowed to dry. The edge is glued and fitted to the stanchions. You will notice the brass pins in the deck. They are set into blocks glued under the deck. One is for the aft bollard and the other two are for the davits. While I was waiting for the glue to dry, I added bollards and fenders according to the plan.

This is the interface that mates the forward cabin to the deck. You can use your own ingenuity here. I do it because it is easier to work on the cabins as separate pieces than it is to build them on the deck.

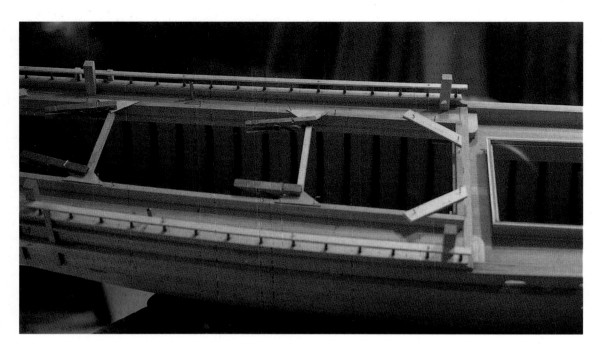

This is the interface structure for the engine house. It will be removed to build the actual structure.

The forward wall of the engine house.

The rear wall has been added and support for the side walls incorporated. This piece is wide in order to eliminate tearing and splitting when the portholes are drilled.

The side walls are complete.

The engine house is sanded smooth and bracing to preserve the shape is added. The structure is now mated to the hull to assure a good fit. Both the bottom edge of the house and the rail on the deck are trimmed as necessary.

Edge trim at the bottom of the house is carefully pinned and glued.

Siding is applied to the forward cabin.

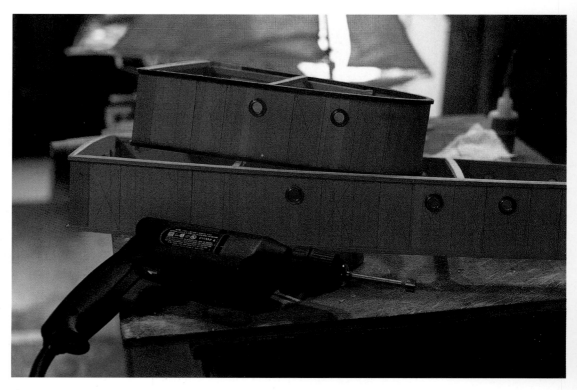

The locations of the door and portholes are plotted and the porthole openings are drilled. The brass portholes are glued in place.

There are a lot of steps in this picture. The forward cabin roof has been attached and reinforcement is added around the edge. The pilot house has been laid out and the bottom rails glued in place. The dark bent poplar pieces were prepared in advance for building the pilot house. I have a small jig that I pin them to that matches the curve of the pilot house.

The framework of the pilot house is erected.

The roof of the engine house is applied and reinforcement added inside and out.

41

Edge trim is added to the engine house.

These are the 24 doors required. They were laid out on a single plywood sheet, the rails and stiles glued and weighted down. When they were dry, I cut them apart and sanded them to dimension.

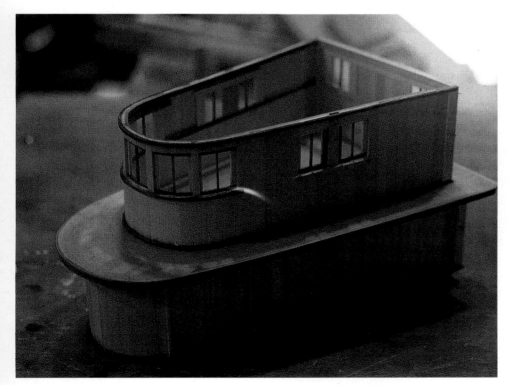

The pilot house structure is completed. You can see how the poplar pieces are used. The windows are built inside the structure. Stops for the sliding doors are now added to both houses. Before adding the roof I paint the house inside and out and glaze the windows. The "glazing" is plastic cordfile material lightly frosted with steel wool.

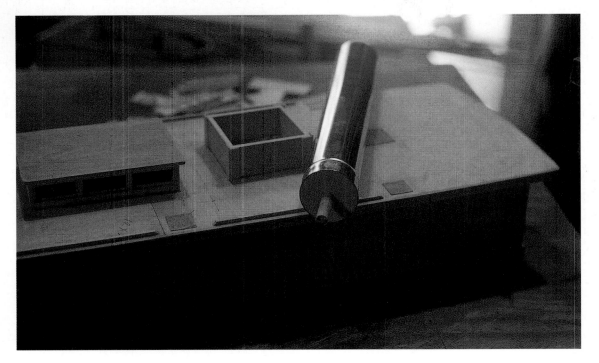

These are all the details of the engine house. The engine stack is 1-1/2" extension tube. The dowel fits in a block glued to the underside of the roof. The pads are for guy lines to the stack and the hand rails are a last minute suggestion from a menhaden boat crewman. He said they were needed to move fore and aft on the boat when underway. I use aluminum duct tape to simulate sections on the stack. When steel wooled, the aluminum looks like steel.

This is the engine house with the sliding doors installed. The track that doors slide on is 1/8" brass angle. Drill small holes for pins, and glue with CCA glue.

While the work on the deck houses dries, I finish remaining details on the hull, including adding a stem liner forward that will be trimmed into a mooring post/bollard, and an additional log rail.

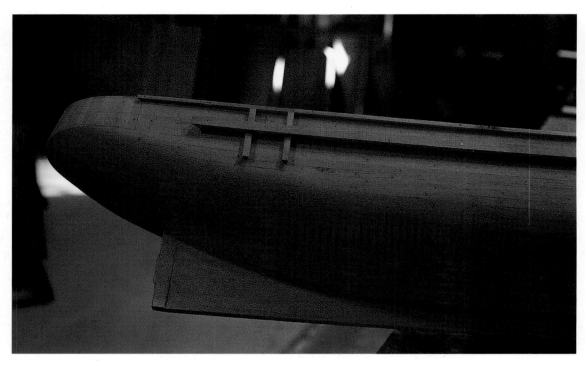

The fenders shown here were installed earlier while waiting for the deck structures to dry.

The crows nest on the boat is rectangular...

and simply built.

The mast assembly is planed down from slightly oversized square stock. Make your fittings from thin metal, then solder, drill, attach and paint prior to fitting to the hull. Not shown is an 1/8" dowel peg at the bottom that inserts through the deck into a block.

The boat is now painted and sanded. It is better to do this before assembly because afterwards painting clean edges inside obstructions is almost impossible. Each house and the hull were painted separately, then glued in place. The stanchions and rails on the pilot house were also painted prior to installation. This picture shows the fitting of the center support for the main hatch. The roof of the forward cabin has been cut away for the mast.

A NOTE ABOUT
PAINT COLORS

Each fleet had different color schemes for their boats. The fleet from Taft Beach, Virginia, painted their boats with black hulls, green superstructure, and white trim. The traditional color scheme is a black hull with dull red superstructure. In Lewes, after a one years experiment with many colors, the Smith Company decided white was best for their wood fleet and black and tan for the new steel boats. The painting process consisted of masking off the windows with plywood panels and letting the paint fly. The wooden boat fleet at Lewes became known as the "White Fleet."

The weathering you see on the model is achieved using an airbrush and thin acrylic washes of black and rust. The boat is soaked with clean water before washes are applied, and afterwards clean water is used to wash away excess color.

Small metal details are now added, such as eyes for the stack and door handles.

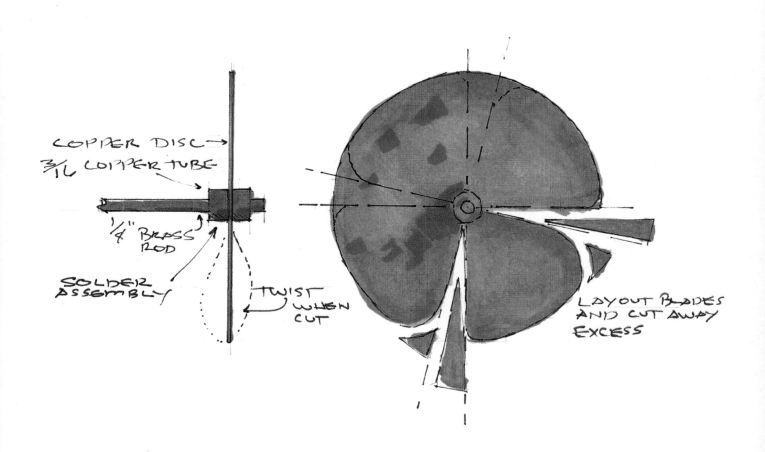

COPPER DISC
3/16 COPPER TUBE

1/4" BRASS ROD

SOLDER ASSEMBLY

TWIST WHEN CUT

LAYOUT BLADES AND CUT AWAY EXCESS

The propeller is made by cutting a circle out of thin sheet of copper or other
metal, then cutting the blades and bending them into position.

The name board supports are added to the pilot house roof and the stove chimney is installed. The windows were glued inside the house after the interior was sprayed black and the roof exterior was painted. The roof was attached at the end.

The mast need not be glued. The rigging won't allow it to move. The brace is holding it in position prior to starting the rigging process.

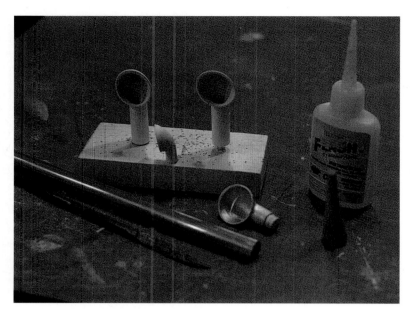

These ventilators were late in arriving so they were added at this point. The bell is white metal cleaned up and glued into the appropriate length of brass tubing. They are painted white.

This is a series of photos that allow you to see the finished model and the rigging. The lift line operated by the winch inside the forward part of the engine house is tied off to a cleat on the mast. A line to swing the boom ties off at the amidships bollard.

The davits are made up from 1/8" copper tubing with 3/16" copper sleeves on the bottom. Metal straps allow attachments of blocks and supports.

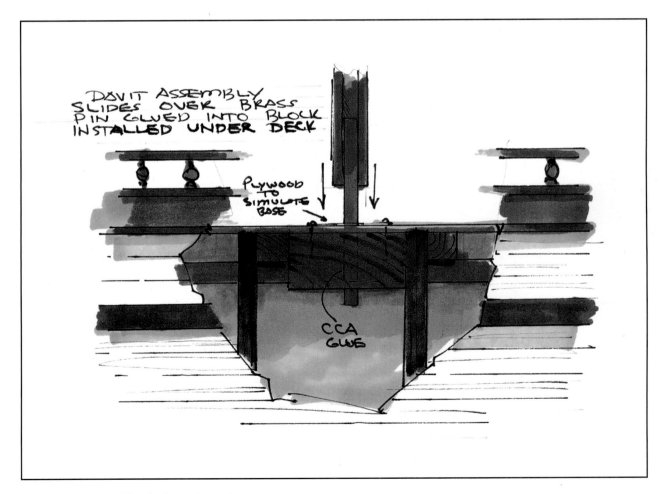

DAVIT ASSEMBLY SLIDES OVER BRASS PIN GLUED INTO BLOCK INSTALLED UNDER DECK

PLYWOOD TO SIMULATE BASE

CCA GLUE

The davit construction.

Stern light.

Mast rigging and ratlines.

Pilot house, forward and starboard.

Pilot house, forward and port.

Pilot house, port

Engine house, port.

Engine house, toward stern.

Stern view, showing the propeller and the rudder.

PARTING SHOTS

This is a photo of what may be the last surviving wooden menhaden boat.
The structure amidships is obviously part of the restaurant dining room and
was not part of the original boat. Still, you can get a feel for the size and
look of these boats. There has been damage to the stem.

Most of the hull is covered in a foam cocoon, but is still recognizable. The stern is laid up in log fashion, pinned and adzed into shape. The davits are not original, neither is the aft door in the engine house.

You can see how narrow these boats are. McKeever Brothers was built in 1911. At the time of this writing the boat was 88 years old.

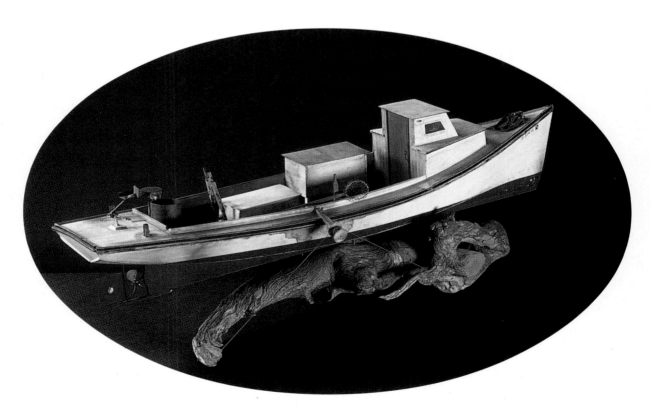